MANUEL A. JUÁREZ

6 Steps to Reclaim Your Time & Finances

Demystifying the Path to Financial Independence

Contents

1

Introduction

Congratulations! I am really excited to know you had the courage to pick up this book. In this book I will share strategies you can begin to explore and implement immediately as you may or may not still have a W-2 job. The reason for writing this book is I had never realized how many ways one can generate income. My desire is to share the different ways people can make a living, and my personal experiences on what has or has not worked for my lifestyle. One of the biggest gifts we have in life is the act of 'exposure'. Or another way to look at this is once you can see one cannot unsee. I hope this book inspires you to create a new stream of income that will get you closer to your financial goals.

A little bit about myself… I have been a commission salesperson the majority of my career. I started B2B product sales in 2007. It was a time similar to now (June 2023) when things seemed very uncertain and no one really knew how things were going to turn out. In fact, as I look back to 2007 it was the time when the two largest hedge funds failed. Fast forward 16 years and we have witnessed another fallout from Silicon Valley Bank. It seems time and time again the cycles of our financial markets go up and down. As I progressed through my career I had the privilege to work with many top Fortune 100 companies such as Uber, Google, Apple, and LinkedIn to name a few. Time and time again I worked very hard to get these customers to use my products and worked even harder to implement my products on their procurement standards. This would provide me with a sense of security, as they continued to use my products over and over again. The commissions would continue to hit my pocket book. My experience has been great as I reflect on all the various projects and the products I represented used at many of these companies.

In March 2020, COVID-19 officially entered our lives and if you paid close attention this phenomenon was activated in late 2019, which is why they call it COVID-**19**. For someone like myself, a sales person whose main job is to solicit people in person and introduce our product highlights. It all came to a stop. Personally, the silver lining was my daughter being born on March 14th, 2020 one day after the official workplace shut down. However, after being at home for what many believed to be only a couple of weeks it turned out to be more than one could really wish for. In fact, many of the social activities we enjoyed had all come to a halt, but more importantly the usual client visits were no longer viable. It was strange.

I quickly recognized how I had all my eggs in one basket. This triggered my exploration to learn new ways to generate income beyond my primary stream of my W-2. I had never given much thought to what else I could do but given the time I had to pivot. I started to do my research on many sites in an attempt to learn as much about passive income. I came across a book called, *Rich Dad, Poor Dad, by Robert Kiyosaki*. This book had been recommended to me about 10 years ago,

I had neglected to read it for no particular reason. It blew my mind! I had gone to college as I was told to do, pursued and completed my MBA and here I was trying to figure out a way to create more income for myself - I was confused. I only knew one way but that finally all changed after being exposed to how the 1% percenters future proof themselves. I studied the various ways one can generate income by the famous Robert Kiyoskai Income Quadrant: Employee, Business Owner, Self-employed and Investor.

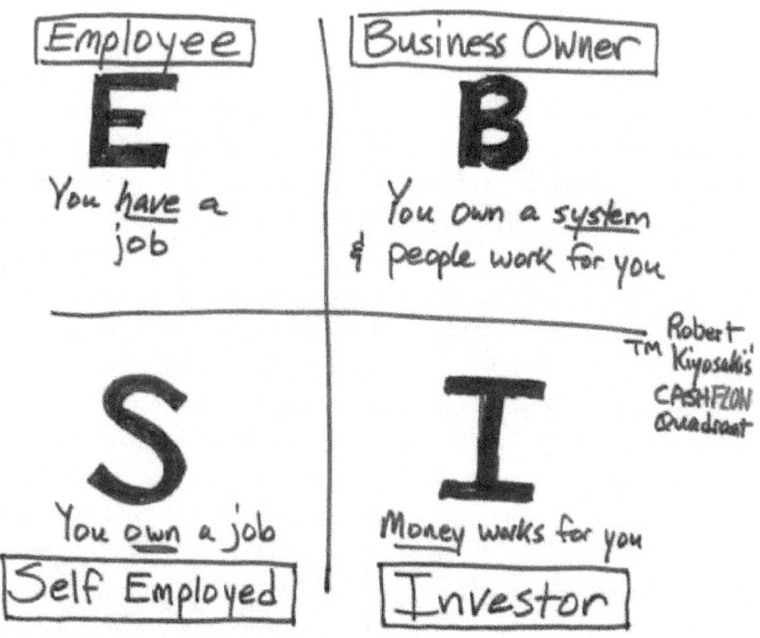

The quadrant framework marked a turning point in my professional trajectory, prompting a shift in how I approached my daily work. This realization prompted me to seek a more robust positioning, a strategic stance that would empower me to adeptly navigate the new wave of potential future disruption. The need for change was undeniable; I recognized the imperative to shift from one quadrant to another, redefining my approach and augmenting my resilience in the face of evolving circumstances.

I trust the information in this book can demystify the journey of financial independence and provide insight on passive income strategies to secure your future. Whether you've thought about it or not it is possible.

2

Get Your Mind Right

Getting my mind right has been the biggest challenge as I embarked on the exploration of passive income. I had been conditioned to believe income can only be generated through hard work and at times it also meant doing things we don't truly love. We all start going to school around the age of 5. We get placed in environments at an early age where someone else guides us to be safe, develop socially accepted norms and be part of the group. I suppose this is acceptable since as little people we need guidance until we enter adulthood. Then we either go to college, get a decent paying job and others decide to join the service - thank you. Time and time again this process continues to be normalized in our society today. It is a cycle many of us are comfortable with and pass to others as the socially acceptable path.

However, this path does not allow us to think for ourselves or explore new ways to do things. If we are commonly guided by this path how can one think for themselves? How does one recondition themselves to believe new methods exist? In 2022, the U.S. Patent office published 418,123 patent applications along with 360,625 published patents granted. This validates the fact there is a group of individuals who believe new things can be introduced in our markets. This data alone proves that believing a new way of doing things is possible. Everyday we all experience something we know can be approached and solved in a different way. Yet many neglect to lean into this perspective. Why? Why is it easier to keep on the path others have been through and instead create our own paths. For me this continues to be a struggle because our society, whether we believe or not , is systemized by external factors. The only action we can control is what we decide to do for ourselves.

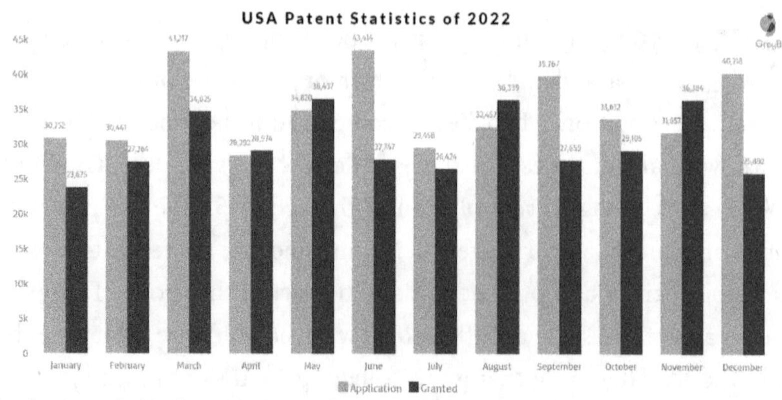

It is critical to recondition our minds and unlearn many of the beliefs which have guided us in our paths to reach the stage of our journey today. Without this realization one cannot pursue a new way of doing anything. It all starts in your mind. It has been tremendously helpful to find resources such as books, audiobooks, podcasts, meetups and webinars where you learn from individuals who are actively doing things differently. There is always another way to do things, and it gives us control over the mental fears which sabotage our dreams and goals. Finding a local network is even better as I have learned from many of them, and how their mental hurdles were ones they had to overcome at some point in their lives. The same mentors I have looked up to also had insecurities, doubts and self imposed beliefs. Yet they were overcome by surrounding themselves by resources that validated their new beliefs and the direction of the new journey.

As you begin to pursue your new future, realize this version of yourself is different. It is smarter, feels more comfortable asking for help but more importantly has ownership of the *super power* strength and leans on others to supplement what you do need. What is your *Superpower*? This can often be defined as experience in any subject matter that you're naturally good at. Or a specialty you know so much it comes natural to the point you can teach others. Oftentimes our super power is undervalued because it comes so easy to do. Yet the same skill set that is easy for one person may be a big challenge for another. Think about 5-10 things you genuinely enjoy doing? It does not have to be in a professional setting, it can be anything you enjoy doing. Once you can identify this you will be able to break down the principle and apply it to specific areas of your life.

Once you begin to operate from this new lens you will begin to see progress much faster. The resistance of not allowing us to do something new is the same reason changes in our lives are difficult to implement and sustain in the long run. Recognizing the resistance is what is needed to push through any new challenge one is experiencing. Once we push through it the new version of ourselves gains confidence and we begin to grow mentally. If we do this over and over again we quickly realize how our fears can easily be cured by action.

3

What is Passive Income?

Passive income refers to money earned with minimal or no active effort once the initial setup is done. It is commonly combined with other sources of income such as regular employment or side hustle.

An example of passive income is rental income or any other activity where the owner is not active in the business. Depending on the type of income you would like to set up, timing will vary since most strategies require the effort to be front loaded. However, when done strategically the effort can be a great way to establish financial independence and even early retirement, since the beneficiary will continue to receive income whether the owner remains active in creating the revenue.

Passive income is not always a lump sum payout, like the sale of a home or stock payout. It can come from a source that is paid out over a period of time yet not always guaranteed. The biggest advantage of passive income is when done strategically the payouts can be received for multiple years and even across generations. This is where the term *generational wealth* comes in, which is the ability to conserve and maintain these streams of income from one generation to the next.

There are several sources of passive income which can supplement your regular day job. But it is very important to understand the mechanics of each option before embarking on the path that best suits your lifestyle and short/long term goals. Below are several common options typically advised by the common institutional advisors.

Deposits:

Deposits are a common way to generate passive income. You keep a certain amount of money in a bank account, and over time, the bank pays you interest on your savings. The interest rate is set by the type of deposit account you choose. Depending on the bank of choice *deposit* rates at the time this book was written ranged between 0.01% - 4.75%.

One popular type of deposit account is called a Certificate of Deposit (CD). With a CD, you agree to keep a specific amount of money in the bank for a fixed period of time. CDs usually offer higher interest rates compared to regular savings accounts, which can be attractive to people looking to invest. If you have more money to deposit and are willing to keep it in the bank for a longer time, you might earn an even higher interest rate. Depending on the bank of choice *CD* rates at the time this book was written ranged between 4.50% (5 year hold term) - 5.60% (1 year hold term).

Bank deposits are a safe and stable option for passive income. While they may not make you rich quickly, they are considered low-risk investments. So, if safety is a top priority for you, bank deposits can be a good choice. You will most likely need to compare two to three options to make sure you are comfortable with the hold periods. But more importantly how quickly you can access the funds if for any reason you need the funds back.

Stocks:

Stocks are a popular and promising way to build wealth through passive income. When you own shares of a company's stock, you can make money in two ways: First, when the value of the company grows, the price of its stock increases, and you can sell it for a profit. Second, some companies share their profits with their shareholders by paying dividends.

Investing in stocks can be risky because stock prices can go up and down quickly based on changes in the market. Some stocks, called value stocks, can be especially uncertain and risky for future earnings.

However, the advantage of investing in stocks is that you can diversify your investments, spreading your money across different companies. This can help reduce the risk if some stocks don't perform well. Stocks also have the potential for significant growth, often outperforming other types of investments.

For example, the average return of the stock market has been around 14.8% per year for the S&P 500 Index. This potential for higher returns can attract people who are willing to take risks and want to earn extra income.

Bonds:

Bonds are like loans that you can make to different organizations, like governments or companies. When you buy a bond, you're lending them money. A bond has a few important parts: the price you paid for it, the face value (which is the amount they will pay you back), the coupon rate (which is the interest rate), the coupon date (when you get paid the interest), and the maturity date (when they pay you back the full amount).

As a bond holder, you'll get regular interest payments, which is a stable way to earn passive income. You can also sell your bond to someone else before it matures, which might let you make some extra money if the bond's value goes up. Bonds are generally safer than stocks because they don't change as much with market ups and downs. However, they also don't give as high returns as stocks.

Rental Income & Royalties:

Rental income and royalties are two types of passive income. Rental income is when someone pays you regularly to use your property or space. For example, if you own an apartment and someone rents it from you, the rent they pay is your rental income. It's a great way to earn money without doing much work, but you need to buy the property first, which can be expensive unless you have access to (PPM) *private placement memorandum* which are usually exclusive and/or only offered to accredited investors.

Royalties are payments you receive when someone uses something you own, like a song, book, or invention. For instance, if you wrote a book, you might earn money every time someone buys a copy. Royalties can add up over time and provide a steady income.

The good thing about rental income and royalties is that you have more control over your investments compared to other passive income sources. With rental properties, you can manage and take care of them directly or indirectly. However, keep in mind that even though it's passive income, being a landlord might still involve some occasional work, like finding tenants or handling repairs.

Digital Products:

Digital products have revolutionized the investment market and many other industries thanks to modern technologies. These products can include things like online courses, e-books, software, and digital art. The best part is that once you create and set them up, they can generate passive income for you without much ongoing effort.

Selling digital products is a great way to earn money while doing something you love. For example, if you're good at photography, you can sell your digital photos online. Or if you have expertise in a particular subject, you can create an online course and teach others. The possibilities are endless, and the internet allows you to reach a global audience.

With digital products, you don't have to worry about manufacturing, shipping, or physical inventory. It's a low-cost and scalable way to generate income. While it may take some time and effort to create the products initially, once they're out there, they can provide a steady stream of passive income, giving you more financial freedom and flexibility in the long run.

4

What is Active Income?

Active income is often considered great for several reasons, as it provides immediate financial benefits and opportunities for personal growth. Here are some of the key advantages of active income:

- *Predictable Earnings*: Active income typically comes from a regular job, freelancing, or running a business where you exchange your time, skills, or services for money. This regular income can provide a sense of stability and predictability, making it easier to budget and plan for expenses.

- *Direct Control*: When you're earning active income, you have direct control over how much you earn. You can actively seek out new opportunities, negotiate higher wages, or take on more clients to increase your income potential.

- *Skill Development*: Many active income sources require you to utilize and enhance your skills, knowledge, and expertise. This constant learning and improvement can lead to personal and professional growth, making you more valuable in the job market.

- *Networking Opportunities*: Engaging in active income activities often involves interacting with clients, customers, colleagues, and other professionals in your field. This can lead to valuable networking connections that might open doors to new opportunities or collaborations.

- *Immediate Financial Gratification*: Unlike passive income, which may take time to build up, active income provides immediate financial rewards. This can be particularly useful for covering day-to-day expenses, emergencies, and short-term financial goals.

- *Structured Work Environment*: Many active income sources involve a structured work environment, such as a job with set working hours. This structure can provide a routine and sense of purpose, which can be beneficial for maintaining productivity and work-life balance.

- *Skills Transferability*: The skills you develop while earning active income can often be transferred to other roles or industries, making you adaptable to changing job markets and career shifts.

- *Personal Fulfillment*: Finding meaning and purpose in your work is important for overall job satisfaction. Active income can provide a sense of accomplishment and fulfillment when you see the results of your efforts directly impacting your income and the success of your work.

- *Faster Financial Progress*: With active income, you have more control over your earning potential. By working harder, improving your skills, and taking on additional responsibilities, you can accelerate your financial progress and achieve your goals faster.

- *Sense of Achievement*: Meeting goals, completing projects, and contributing to the success of your job or business can provide a strong sense of achievement and boost your self-esteem.

However, it's important to note that active income also has its limitations. It often requires a significant time commitment, and your income may be directly tied to the number of hours you work. This can lead to burnout, limit your flexibility, and make it challenging to achieve long-term financial freedom. Balancing active income with passive income (where money is earned with less ongoing effort) can be a wise strategy to achieve a more sustainable financial situation over time.

5

Generational Wealth: Building for the Family's Future

Generational wealth is all about creating a strong financial foundation that can benefit not just you but also your children, grandchildren, and beyond. It means working hard now to set up your family for a brighter and more secure future.

1. *Investing and Saving Smartly*: To build generational wealth, families often invest their money in things like real estate, stocks, or businesses. They also make sure to save a portion of their income for the long term. This way, the money can grow over time and support future generations.

2. *Passing Down Knowledge and Values*: Generational wealth isn't just about money; it's also about passing down important knowledge and values. Families teach their children about money management, investing, and how to make good financial decisions. They also share important life lessons and family values that guide their actions for generations to come.

3. *Reducing Financial Stress for Future Generations*: One of the goals of generational wealth is to reduce financial stress for the next generations. By setting up a strong financial plan, families can provide financial security and opportunities for their children and grandchildren. This may include funding for education, starting businesses, or buying additional real estate.

4. *Long-Term Thinking and Planning*: Generational wealth requires thinking beyond just the present moment. Families make long-term plans and set up legal structures, like trusts, to ensure that their wealth is passed down smoothly and protected for future generations.

5. *Making a Positive Impact on Society*: Families with generational wealth often have the means to give back to their communities and support causes they care about. They can make a positive impact on society by supporting charities, church, education, and other important initiatives.

In short, generational wealth is about working hard, making smart financial choices, and passing down both money and valuable knowledge to benefit your family's future for many generations to come. It's a way to create a lasting legacy and provide opportunities for your descendants to thrive and make a positive impact on the world.

6

Choosing a Lane

The first step to choosing a path is understanding the options available to you. You may already have individuals in your network today who are passive investors. One way to find out is to make a list of all the individuals you know and ask them: *are you a passive investor?*

Oftentimes you will be surprised at the response you receive. One of the investment types I decided to pursue is PPM (Private Placement Memorandum) for apartment syndications. This is when a group of people come together and invest in a larger apartment property that they might not be able to afford on their own. The main advantage is monthly cash flow and long term appreciation. I was once having lunch with a close friend and I shared my new path on how I planned to create passive income. I was extremely surprised when he told me, "once you have a project opportunity - let me know and I will invest". This was a pivotal moment in my passive income journey as you never know where your next supporter or investor will come from.

The following is a list of passive income strategies which (a) have a minimal cost of entry, (b) require minimal effort and experience (c) can provide cash flow (d) others which require substantial cost to enter with advantageous returns.

A= active P= passive	*Annual ROI*	*Cash Flow*	*Level of Experience*	*Risk*	*Min Initial Investment Amount*	*Hold Time*
ATMs *(A)*	20-25 %	20-25%	Low	Medium	$5,000	Up to you
Apartment Syndication (A)	NA	No cap	High	High	$0-$50K (Can use 401K)	3-10 years
Apartment Syndication (P)	20%	8-12%	Low	Low	$50K (Can use 401K)	3-10 years
Commercial Retails Parks (P)	20%	8%	Low	Medium	$100K	10 years +
Hotel Development (P)	18-25%	NA	Low	Medium	$250K	1-3 years
Hotel Development (A)	No cap	NA	High	Medium	NA	1-3 years
House & Land Flipping	40-60%	NA	High	High	$40K	Up to you
Medical Office Buildings (P)	12%	4%	Low	Low	$100K	10 years +
Mobile Home Parks	20%	8%	Low	Medium	$20-50K	10 years +
Mobile Home Rental	20-25%	20-25%	High	Low	$5k	Up to you
Storage Units (A)	20%	10%	Low	Low	$20-50K	10 years +
Private Real Estate Fund (P)	10-15%	10-15%	Medium	Medium	$25-50K	5-7 years

7

Take ACTION!

Taking action is the catalyst for achieving any goal, whether it's related to income streams, career, health, or personal development. Overcoming self-imposed beliefs, fear, and the unknown is a crucial step in this journey. Here are three main ways to take action and overcome these obstacles:

1. **Challenge Self-Imposed Beliefs**: Many of us carry limiting beliefs that hold us back from pursuing our goals. These beliefs often stem from past experiences or societal conditioning. To overcome them:

- *Identify Limiting Beliefs*: recognize and write down the beliefs that are holding you back. Are they based on evidence or assumptions?
- *Question the Beliefs*: challenge the validity of these beliefs. Are they really true, or are they just assumptions? What evidence contradicts these beliefs?
- *Reframe Beliefs*: replace limiting beliefs with empowering ones. Instead of saying "I can't do this," say "I am capable of learning and

growing in this area."

2. **<u>Embrace Fear and the Unknown</u>**: Fear is a natural response to the unfamiliar,

but it can also be a sign that you're stepping out of your comfort zone and growing.

To embrace fear and overcome it:

- *Recognize Fear as Growth*: understand that fear often accompanies growth and new experiences. It's a sign that you're pushing your boundaries.
- *Break It Down*: divide big goals into smaller, manageable steps. Taking one small step at a time can make the unknown seem less daunting.
- *Focus on Learning*: instead of fixating on potential failure, shift your focus to what you'll learn from the experience, regardless of the outcome.

3. **<u>Desire, Belief, and Action</u>**: Desire, belief, and action form a powerful trifecta for

achieving your goals. Each element builds upon the other:

- *Desire*: Clarify what you truly want to achieve. What drives you? Having a strong desire will fuel your motivation to take action.
- *Belief*: Cultivate a deep belief in your ability to succeed. Visualize yourself reaching your goals and achieving success.
- *Action*: Take consistent, deliberate steps toward your goal. Break down your actions into manageable small tasks and commit to regular progress. Whether you spend 30 minutes or 3 hours per day. Your daily action will create momentum.

Your personal milestones, from completing grammar school to graduating high school to completing your graduate program and starting a family, are a testament to the power of desire, belief, and action. Each of these accomplishments required overcoming challenges, embracing fear, and taking consistent steps toward your goals.

Remember that growth and transformation happen outside of your comfort zone. By embracing fear and taking action despite it, you open yourself up to new experiences, skills, and opportunities. Your journey is a testament to the fact that achieving your goals is not just about dreaming and believing, but also about the proactive steps you take to turn those dreams into reality.

8

Conclusion

In conclusion, we have explored a wide range of passive investing strategies in the real estate market. We've delved into various avenues to uncover the potential for generating passive income and building wealth through strategic investments.

Throughout the chapters, we've seen that passive investing can offer unique advantages and opportunities for both seasoned investors and those new to the field. Each investment type has its own set of pros and cons, catering to different risk tolerances and financial goals.

One common theme that emerged from all the discussions is the power of collaboration. Whether it's through apartment syndication, commercial retail parks, or private real estate funds, pooling resources and expertise with like-minded investors can unlock access to larger and more lucrative opportunities. Additionally, having knowledgeable and experienced support systems play a crucial role in achieving success in any of your investment goals.

We've learned that passive investing doesn't mean a complete hands-off approach. While it allows investors to earn income without day-to-day involvement, careful due diligence, ongoing monitoring, and informed decision-making remain vital aspects of any successful passive investment strategy. As you embark on your passive investing journey, it's essential to recognize that each investment opportunity requires a thorough understanding of the mechanics, associated risks, and potential rewards. Diversifying your investment portfolio across different asset classes can further enhance stability and resilience in the face of market fluctuations. By applying the knowledge gained from this book, you can position yourself to capitalize on passive investing opportunities, potentially securing a steady stream of passive income and paving the way towards long-term financial success.

Remember to consult with financial advisors and/or industry experts to tailor your approach and make informed choices that align with your unique circumstances and aspirations. Happy investing!

If you found any of this information valuable I kindly ask if you left a favorable review for the book on Amazon!

9

Resources

Cain, S. L. (2023, July 18). 10 Passive income ideas for 2023 · TIME stamped. *TIME Stamped.* https://time.com/personal-finance/article/passive-income-ideas/

Carson, C. (2020, August 31). *The cashflow quadrant explained - how you earn income matters.* Coach Carson. https://www.coachcarson.com/cash-flow-quadrant-how-earn-matters/

Goldberg, M. (2023a). What is the average interest rate for savings accounts? *Bankrate.* https://www.bankrate.com/banking/savings/average-savings-interest-rates/

Goldberg, M. (2023b). Best CD Rates for August 2023 - Up to 5.61% | Bankrate. *Bankrate.* https://www.bankrate.com/banking/cds/cd-rates/

James Royal, Ph.D. (2023). 23 passive income ideas to help you make money in
2023. *Bankrate.* https://www.bankrate.com/investing/passive-income-ideas/

Rich Dad's CASHFLOW Quadrant: Rich Dad's Guide to Financial Freedom:
Kiyosaki, Robert T.: 9781612680057: Amazon.com: Books. (n.d.).
https://www.amazon.com/Rich-Dads-CASHFLOW-Quadrant-Financial/dp/161268054

Shapiro, B. E. a. D. (2010). Transform your fear into courage. *Oprah.com.*
https://www.oprah.com/spirit/transform-your-fear-into-courage/all

USA patent trends and statistics in 2022 - Insights;Gate. (2023, March 22).
Insights;Gate. https://insights.greyb.com/usa-patents-stats-of-2022/

Wikipedia contributors. (2023). Passive income. *Wikipedia.*
https://en.wikipedia.org/wiki/Passive_income